T0353751

THIS IS MY
STORY

If You Know God No Explanation
is necessary, If You Don't Know God
No Explanation Is Possible

PASTOR HEATHER LYNN

Copyright © 2016 Pastor Heather Lynn.

All rights reserved. No part of this book may be used or reproduced by any means, graphic, electronic, or mechanical, including photocopying, recording, taping or by any information storage retrieval system without the written permission of the author except in the case of brief quotations embodied in critical articles and reviews.

WestBow Press books may be ordered through booksellers or by contacting:

WestBow Press
A Division of Thomas Nelson & Zondervan
1663 Liberty Drive
Bloomington, IN 47403
www.westbowpress.com
1 (866) 928-1240

Because of the dynamic nature of the Internet, any web addresses or links contained in this book may have changed since publication and may no longer be valid. The views expressed in this work are solely those of the author and do not necessarily reflect the views of the publisher, and the publisher hereby disclaims any responsibility for them.

Any people depicted in stock imagery provided by Thinkstock are models, and such images are being used for illustrative purposes only.
Certain stock imagery © Thinkstock.

ISBN: 978-1-5127-3640-3 (sc)
ISBN: 978-1-5127-3641-0 (e)

Print information available on the last page.

WestBow Press rev. date: 06/08/2016

WESTBOW
PRESS®
A DIVISION OF THOMAS NELSON
& ZONDERVAN

I could not understand why one of my co-workers starred at me all the time, we knew he had a girlfriend it was strange, I tried not to notice, finally he came over to me and introduced himself, he invited me to his church, I told him I would love to. I was having problems in my marriage, I needed help, I went on Sunday, he was not there, a nice couple introduced themselves, Betty and John, the first thing she ask me was is your husband lost? I didn't know what she meant, but I did say yes, after service we exchange numbers, they called the next day and gave me scriptures to read and invited me back to church. We were getting to know each other better. I did go to church with them a few more times. She started calling every day, she wanted to know about my situation at home, I was so happy to have someone to talk to. My husband wasn't working, he was very depressed, and he would take his frustration out on me in many different ways. My daughter was just a little girl, that's what hurt the most seeing her right in the mist of it. I was in a state of mind where I could not help myself; it had taken its toll on me. Betty and John wanted to meet my husband; they came over and tried to help him. John would take my husband to work with him and bring the paycheck to me to pay bills, that was a blessing, we had car trouble, they let us use their car, Betty took my daughter swimming at her house, she had a fellowship meeting, and they blessed me with money to pay bills, they were wonderful people, she would always ask me to say this prayer, it seems like every time she ask I would make an excuse or walk away, she never pressured me, she would let it go. I was home and I felt very tired, I leaned against the wall and said, I can't take this anymore. I got in my car and started driving, I didn't know where I was going, but I knew I was not going to Betty's she will ask me to say that prayer, and I just don't want to, the next thing I know, I was pulling up in Betty's driveway, I got out of the car, walked to her front door and It opened, Betty was standing right there, as if she knew I was coming, she say are you ready, I knew what she meant, I said yes, she says come and sit right here, I sat on her couch, she say repeat after me, this is what I said. God forgive me of my sins, come into my life, I believe Jesus died for us amen. I could not move for a while, I felt calm and peaceful, relieved, she gave me a big hug, and I went back home. I didn't feel the same. I had no fear. I started taking better care of my daughter. I could see things better than before. John and Betty didn't come around much after that. I believe they were on a mission for God, and their job was complete. They never stop loving, and that is what won me over to God. He loved me first, and there is no greater love. He is the beginning and the end. I was in so much pain, I could not see a way out, but God sent two gardening angels, to lead me to him for peace and rest. I started going to revival almost every night, I was hungry and thirsty for more of God. A powerful pastor will preach tonight. I had to be there. He started to pray, he ask all to come up front if there was room, the place was crowed, if not he say just stay where you are and receive, there was no room left, I stayed at my seat, standing as he was praying, I felt warmth from my head to my feet, I knew God was cleansing me, and covering me with his blood, it seems like my husband saw a difference in me, he was not attacking me anymore. I ask God what I could do to give back for the peace he has given me, and he said very plane, go to the nursing home and visit the elderly. The next day I went to the nearby nursing home. I was very shy; I drove around it three times before I got out of the car. Finally, I parked went in and talk to the nurse, and I told her why I was there. She welcomed me, and gave me papers to fill out. This is God I know, because I was never patient. I would go on Saturdays and stay all day. It was hard to get away from some of them I tried to go in every room. One lady was very elegant and beautiful. She was married to a doctor; she would talk about her life as his wife. She loved it, I enjoyed her; no one visits her. She was very lonely. I notice in a matter of six months, she started deteriorating down to nothing. She stops talking. It was sad to see. There were many different personalities there, one little lady just wanted a smile. I would take my daughter with me some times. She loved my daughter, some wanted to talk girl talk, one man in a wheelchair was making passes at me he was funny. I loved them all. I did that for one year. I went to revival almost every night I needed more of God. A few months later, my husband had a heart attack and passed away. God put a call on my life shortly after that. The First thing he said to do, was get rid of everything you own. I go wow, I just bought some new things, and I worked hard to get them, are you sure that's what you really mean? It's like he said, I will prove it. I had a fairly new car, I'm driving down the road, and the car stopped, I pulled over to the side. A man stop to help, he said ma'am your engine is gone. I had the car towed to the shop. I get a call from my daughter; she tells me she just got a ticket for two hundred dollars. I get home, and I say God what have I done, he said to read judges 2-2, something about not doing what I told you to do. I got on the phone and call everyone to come, and get what they wanted, and just give me whatever you have, until it was all gone. My daughter was so sweet about it all, and she didn't fully understand. One of the girls I worked with invited me to her church for a special woman's meeting; I went with her on a Thursday night, a lot of beautiful talented ladies and pastors were there. My friend wanted me to tell my testimony. I was very shy, I refuse to do it. I didn't know what to say, but she wouldn't let it go, so I did go up, and I'm glad I did, because whatever God told me to say, touched them. At the end everyone went up to the prayer line. I sat in a chair against the wall agreeing in prayer; all of a sudden, I felt a hand touch my shoulder. A pretty lady said to me, God says he has not forgotten you. And there's something he want you to do. If you fast and pray he will reveal it to you. I went to my church on Sunday. I was catholic at the time. Mass was just about over, and I'm all into Jesus, and I started crying, I get up walk to my car crying. Get inside the car, I can't stop crying, and I here God say, you are going to go all over the world and tell your story. I go what story. I'm from Alabama, I can't talk, who's going to listen to me, besides I am very shy I just can't do that.

He said once again you are going to go all over the world and tell you story. What story anyway I said. He said very bold like. You are going to go all over the world and tell your story. And no you can't, you will open your mouth and I will put the words in it. And I said ok God whatever you say. I'm still crying all day Monday. Tuesday he said and you are going to dance for me also. There is not enough of it. I said hold on now, I wanted to be a dance teacher or dancer when I was twenty years old not now, and then I said, ok God whatever you say' I stopped crying after that. I was in a daze for a few days. The same lady invited me back to her ladies meeting they have monthly. I was happy to go back. This time a powerful pastor was there; the message was very uplifting. and now she started to prophesy. She come right to me, and this is what she said, come here sister come here, I get up and run to her. She say go from her go from her, she's going to be used of God. He's going to make you whole tonight, are you ready for this? I fell to the floor, passed out, after I got myself together, we started to leave, as I was walking to my car a man come running behind me, he say miss you need to get that tape, you are going to Spain, Germany, and Mexico He ask me do you have money. I will buy it for you. I went back inside and bought the tape, and this is what the prophet said, go from her go from her, God's going to make you whole tonight, are you ready for this, I prophesize over her from the book of Nahum, it will not come back a second time, she is going to be use of God, generational curses will be broken, the blood of Jesus is against you, she will go into some deep dark places where others dare to go, but God has equipped you for such a time as this, you're going to Mexico, Germany, Spain, London will open up for you to preach the articles of God. And she said, you better give God some praise in this place, to all of us. I was in a daze for some time after that, but there was no slowing down, it is amazing how God used different people in my life for his glory. I met a man at the mall, we talked about different churches, and he tells me his pastor is good about helping baby pastors get their ministries started. He ask me to visit next Sunday, and I did, the pastor was very open about helping, he let me speak, he made me feel very comfortable, I stayed at the church for a month, they love my dancing. my last Sunday there, I was leaving almost out the door, a lady come running behind me, she go ma'am excuse me, but I am supposed to help you, and teach you. God is telling me this, just like that, and it all fell into place, I was under her ministry for one year. A Powerful women of God, Kind and patient, after she ordained me we went our separate ways, I'm sure our paths will cross again. God took me aside, to himself for one year and taught me everything I know. I never understood the Bible until I gave my life to God and now I quote scripter and look the verses and chapters up later. God said to me, I want you to go to the homeless shelters and minister; you will have to live there in order to feel their needs. I thought me go to the shelters, wow, the very next day pastor that ordained me came over, and said God want you to go to the shelters now. I never told her one thing about it. My daughter had left for college. I went the next day to the shelter down town. I was so nervous I walked up to the front desk, introduced myself as Pastor Heather. God has sent me here to help. The lady said you are welcome. There are so many battered women here. I filled out paper work. And I went on a tour of the place. It was late and everyone was coming in for the night. No one is allowed inside during the day. Everyone was getting in line for dinner. We sat at a big table. I was very nervous. This one girl said to me, I'm going to sit with you; my husband beat me, and made me leave the house. I was so nervous I got up and moved away from the table. The next day I realized what I had done. I felt so bad. I ask God to forgive me. I am so sorry. And I wonder if I was being too hard on myself. I didn't have time to think before she came to me. It took me a long time to overcome that. And I promise God I would never do it again. After dinner we went to our dorms for the night. Before I could find my way, a lady just released from jail walked in. she came right to me, put her head on my shoulder, crying and telling me all about her problems. Now I could see I have no time to waste. Some of the girls had weapons. Two lesbians ask me to marry them. One lady would wrap herself in plastic every night. The smell was awful. Many would talk to themselves, and answer, but I was able to minister to them, just letting them know someone care, and you are special to God. They have given up and think no one cares. A kind word makes a big difference. You are beautiful. And it's never too late to turn your life around. God loves you so much. Let's pray. They would fall in my arms and cry and give their lives to God. I tell them. You are going to be ok now, you want be in this place much longer. Love never fails. It is what we all need. I say to everyone, if you claim to know God, and you shout yes I'm a Christian. Then act like it, go spread God's love to some hurting person. without love you are bankrupt, One night at bed time this girl asks me if I thought a catholic priest could cast out demons. She looked scary, her voice was changing. She tried to tell me her friend was demon prosiest. Not her, I knew she was the one. All the girls started running away, they were afraid, I wanted to run, it was very scary, but God say stand there. I said to her, I don't know about a catholic priest, but I know who can. I say God can do all things. She kept going on and on changing her voice. Eyes changing, I said to her, I will stand here, and when you are ready let me know, all the girls were standing outside the door looking in. finally she said ok I'm ready. then what I said to her was, the sinners prayer, she repeated after me, and she grabbed me, and would not let go, finally, she got in her bed and fell asleep, she woke up the next morning, and we thought we were looking at a different person, she look like an angel, all the girls came running to me saying, We will never forget what you did as long as we live. We cannot believe it. After the girl left I sat down with everybody and explain to them that I did nothing. God cast out the demons from her not me. I'm just like you, and God wanted you to see that, to let you know whatever you are going though he can take care of your situation. Nothing's too big for God. By this time twelve people had given their lives to God. There was one little eighteen year old boy I started talking to. He didn't have a care in the world. I tried to be a mother figure; he didn't want to listen at all, he would make jokes about everything. On Sundays I could go in the chapel and speak. I ask him, would you please come to church Sunday. He go get serious, I would not set foot in that place. He was wasting his young life on drugs. I know God was going to work it out. I had been working on him for at least a month; it was Sunday we gathered in the chapel for service, at the very end I looked up, and here come the kid that said he would never set foot in this place. You could see my heart beating outside of my cloths. I ran to greet him, and thank him for coming. I ask him if I could pray for him, he accepted the lord. All I could do was, give God the glory. I had been at this shelter for a few months. I was tired. I had ask God how much longer will I be here, but I say after what you did for this kid, God I will stay here the rest of my life. It was a miracle. And I am overwhelmed by your glory amen. It wasn't long after that, God led me to leave. I headed to another state. I had very little money. It is so amazing how God provide everything you need. When I got to my location, I remember sitting at a Wendy's, waiting for God to tell me what to do next. I left to get gas. I ask a young man at the station about the shelter. I told him I was a minister. He wasted no time asking me to pray for him. He said he was not coming this way, but for some reason he changed his mind. His wife is divorcing him and he was taking it very hard. I prayed for him, he held me and cried like a baby. I told him to put God in control of his situation, he will be ok. I left and found the shelter. I didn't stay at that one as long. A few weeks later it was time to leave. I always have my car check before I get on the road. a mechanic looked at my car and said ma'am your front end is loose. I would not advise you to get on the road. I didn't have any extra money, I say God he is saying because the roads are so bad here my front end is loose. God spoke and said, who's telling you to leave. I say you are God. I got on the road headed to where I was lead to go. But I didn't stop there I went to a military base three hours further away. I drove right up to a building call family support. I walked in introduced myself to the lady at the front desk, she ask how did you find us? no one can find this building, but God did amen. I started talking about the problem with my car. She says we can help you, fill out this form. I talk to another lady, she needed me to get an estimate, I did the next day and she wrote a check for the repairs and one for me also, for food and gas. God will supply all of your needs according to his riches and glory. Let not your heart be troubled. He cares for you. My husband retired from the military. I have an ID card, but I had no idea I could go there for car repairs. I went to a flea market looking around. Here comes a man that almost walked into me, I ask how are you he says not to good I go what's wrong, he say ma'am, I'm tired of drinking, I'm homeless . The smell was very strong. I say do you mind if I pray for you? he gave his life to God. And he said lady, he was crying, you don't know how you make me feel. I say you are going to be fine, it's not me. God has set you free. The most beautiful part of it all. I went back to the same flea market one year later. Someone walked up to me and said hello. I had no idea why this person would get in my face, he say don't you remember me? I'm the guy you prayed for a year ago, I go what, all clean and in nice clothes. I say what are you doing? He says I'm the manager here now. I go look what God has done. He gave me a big hug he says the smell of alcohol makes him sick. I say amen glory to God. He's reading his bible, and praying. I have been to many different states ministering in shelters, most of the time with very little money, I would never get lost. I get close, and I might stop and ask for the street address. I rented a mobile home once, I was so tied I just wanted to rest, later I realized a smell that was making me sick, little did I know it was drugs, my car broke down and I was out in the country, I had no money, I had to wait until I got paid, so I was there for one month. I didn't know anyone the houses were two blocks apart. It was not good. I had no one to call. God was right there, he sees everything, so I started to clean the place outside to keep busy, It was in very bad shape, I stayed outside until it was dark, and I tried to sleep in the car at night but the bugs were so bad, that didn't work at all, I never stop praying, God please help me, Lord I will trust you, it doesn't do you any good to complain, it makes it worse, remember the Israelites had to wait 40 years. Paul and Silas were praising the Lord and the prison doors opened amen. God got me through it, when you feel you can't make it call on Jesus, he is all you need amen. He tells us in this world we will have trials and tribulations, but I have overcome the world. I remember I was at a Christian TV station waiting in line to see a powerful minister, and this young girl in front of me starting talking to me, right in the middle she stopped, and say hold it, God is telling me to write you a check. I really want to give people the glory, but I knew God was giving me gas money to get to the next state. her blessing will come from God and she knew that, A lady came behind me as I was leaving another church I visited, and gave me an envelope and said God bless you, later I opened it, there was three hundred dollars in it. If god calls you to a ministry, he will takes care of you, no need to beg or worry, When I'm traveling I stop at a well-lit station and sleep in my car, I go inside and get permission first, and ask them to keep an eye on me. I don't like to drive at night. People come and ask me are you ok do you need anything. another shelter I was in, everybody was sick with bad colds, the worst I have ever seen, the germs were all over, I was able to leave before I got very sick, I did have to go to the hospital and get a shot, I was so tired I never slept in that place, it was the worst of all. A lady came and said to me one night I know you are tired God is going to let you go soon. I was shopping at Wal-Mart one day, and I heard someone say ma am ma am, I turn around and it was a kid, he say you are the most beautiful lady I have ever seen, I say how old are you? He says, I'm nine years old, he had a big patch of hair missing on his head, I ask what happened? he says I had brain surgery, I had cancer, he say in surgery I went to heaven and came back, he told me all about how beautiful it was, and then he started to preach, and glorifying God, his older sister was with him, the parents were shopping around, I did get to meet his parents, they just stud back and watched what God is doing with their baby, they look so happy, and proud of him, and like this is all God not us, praise the lord amen. I was in a coffee shop, and a gentleman walked in, and all I could here was him praising God, I looked up and said amen, he came to my table, and said now I know why I am here, I was going the other direction, but, I was lead here, he told me everything about me that only God could have told him, he prayed for me, and he left just like that, the next shelter I got to, was for children and single mothers, I was sitting by the playground trying to rest, and all the children gather around me, and wanted a hug, I would always try to look after them as best as I could. shelters are not a good place for them, I hadn't flown on a plane in a long time, God knew I was tired, I was flying to my next state, and had the car transported, everything had changed about flying, I had two big bags, and my sign I use when I go on the street and dance. I got up to the ticket counter to check in and I was told I could only take one bag, and I could pay for the other one, the cost was way more than I could afford, so someone called the manager, she came look at my bags, and my sign, she saw I was a minister, she ask someone to get a big box, she put both bags in this big box, she say now one bag and a sign, I just started to cry, I serve a mighty God. he changes hearts, he makes all things possible, I was at the service station getting gas one day, I only had eight dollars, a lady came behind me, she say I notice you aren't getting much gas, she hand me a twenty, and she say will you pray for me, she had no idea who I was, she say I really need prayer, God never cease to amaze me, he met both our needs, I'm in a different town and I always try to find a military base, I feel safe, if I have to sleep in my car. I got to this base and stopped at the BX, it's their shopping mall, God say go meet that vendor, I say do I have to, yes go, I introduced myself I said I just drove in town, he say you must be tired, let my buy lunch, and he did for one week he gave me gas money, now I see why I was sent to him. a very nice man, the favor of God is amazing, I used one of the post offices for general delivery once, and I kid you not every time I walked in the door, there would be long lines, and they would stop and say let me help this lady, they would all do that, two wanted prayer amen, my daughter and I drove a long way to enroll her in college, I sent her in the financial aid office to get everything in order, she came out later and said, mom theirs no money lets go, I say hold on, I went in and said to the lady, we have come a long way, someone is going to do something, she got on her computer, and she go, oh I think we can help you, we will take care of everything for the year, books, food, and your expenses, I thank God, and as we were leaving, the lady looked at my daughter and, said, I have guarding angels watching over me too, all things are possible with God amen. I walked in a store, just to kill time, so I thought, a man came over to me and said, he didn't even say hello, he started talking, I have cancer in my right eye, it's in remission now, if it comes back it will go to my kidney, I know why he came to me, God wants to heal him, I prayed for him, and God will have his way, amen, I got word that my sister had a stroke. I was lead to go be with her. I drove 12 to 13 hour drive, I'm almost here and, God tells me to keep going 2 hours past her city, I drove right on this Air Force Base, I slept in the van that night. The next morning I went to the gym to work out, and take a shower. three men were working at the front counter very fun happy go lucky guys. I introduced myself and told them about my sister, my drive and ministry, the third day I walk in the gym, God say pray for them, so I walked up and told them I need to pray for you guys, they were nice about it, I say you need to take each other's hand, no problem, I begin to pray, and I say repeat after me, they excepted the Lord, and they were looking all around like what just happened, I say you will never be the same, it was their time, and God used me, I never approach anyone, they just come, there is no one like you Lord, and we thank you amen. now it was time to go see my sister. I have prayed for her over and over, I could not reach her, she passed on, I'm thankful I got to see her. This is not our home, God make it very clear we are here to prepare for our eternal home. He tells us to be ready; he is the only one that knows the day or hour he will come, we thank you Lord, for your love, and grace. One lady I met wanted to talk to me about the problems she's having with her teenage son, she's divorced and when her boys go to visit the dad he is abusive to them, she has two sons the oldest one was crying out for help, he was getting into trouble at school, the mother was not giving him much attention, so God came to give them peace, I went over every day being a second mom to them, I called the school and talk to the principal about the situation . all they needed was love, and someone to care, a month of talking and praying and guidance, both boys gave their lives to God. the next court date the judge rule they didn't have to go to visit their dad if they did not want to. The battle is the Lord's take it to him in prayer, now the older boy is doing well, he finished high school and is enrolling in junior college, I say look at God only he could have done that. On my way to another state I needed gas I say what should I do? I looked up and saw a7-11 gas station, behind a sign said church, God say go inside and tell them what you are doing, I walked in, the pastor is standing right there at the door. I go sir I'm a traveling evangelist can you help me with gas please, he say yes because you love the Lord, he walked me to the gas station in front,7-11 and filled my tank up. When God say don't worry he means it. I decided to visit a church for support, so I thought, I know there are some good churches somewhere, I walked in and the eyes started rolling, the first lady was the greeter, she welcomed everyone but me, she passed over me, the pastor started to preach, the first thing he said was, I would never cheat on my wife, standing right in front of me, I go where are their minds, can't be on God never went back. I tried another church pretty much the same. after service I wanted to tell the pastor I enjoyed everything. I looked up and his wife and all her buddies were in a row giving me looks that could kill, I get very irritated when I see people using God for money and social clubs, God is love, he knows and see all things. You do reap what you sow, I went to another base, I was telling one lady a little about my story, she started crying, she say I touched her so much, she say hold on,she left came back with a hand full of money, she had collected from her co-workers, look at God blessing me to keep going, and touched that ladies heart also. the same thing happen at another base, a lady collected money for me, after telling her a little of my story. I lived in this apartment and the word got out that I was a minister, every day I got a knock on my door, for prayer, one lady's blood pressure was out of control I prayed for her, she came back an hour later and say everything was fine, she say God healed her amen. one lady say are you doing this all by my yourself? I go no God is right by my side, he sends his angels, the light that is over me, he talks to me, he gives me signs and visions, he's just using me,he is doing it all, he gets the glory, this happened to me twice, God woke me from my sleep, I heard his voice and I went back to sleep peacefully, he has shown me the man he has chosen to be my husband, this is what he said this is your husband he's not ready yet, he's coming to get you, and no one can have him,and he confirmed it, I saw two rainbows, if he said it he will do it, I just want his will to be done, not mine, I was in one state and getting out of my car my whole left side was numb, I knew something was wrong, I went to the doctor, he sent me to the hospital, all my test was normal except one of my head,they didn't know what the problems was, they released me, and I drove a long way to my home town, with no problem, I went to the doctor as soon as I got there, they couldn't find anything wrong,I went to bed that night, when I got up that morning, I could not move, my left side was numb, I drove back to the hospital and they did a MRI, found out when I was out of town I had a TIA, now they say the MRI shows I have had a massive stroke, all the staff members were my family, I went to take an x-ray, and I said something that touched the technician about God, she yield out amen, and the next thing I know she was in my room. she wanted more of Jesus, The doctor said to me, I expect a full recovery, I say I know because God has already shown me my ministry, and where he is taking me and this is just part of it amen, I was in the hospital for three days, my left side is fine now, God I praise and worship you amen. I have never fit in or been excepted by worldly people, The closer I get to God it gets worse, I am hated by people that know nothing about me, I was invited over for dinner, everyone was talking about things that were not of God, so the minute I got a chance to speak about God, I was ask to leave. I was invited to a meeting, I was a little late, I walked in and the speaker started praying for God not to let any demonic spirits inter the room, and the eyes were rolling from all of them, people are so jealous, and wicked, there is no one to talk to, they try to copy what God has called me to do, I have never been abused so much,the sad part about it is, these are people that are in church, people that are always calming to know God,and will out talk you about him., If It's not about God I can't be around you, I will help you if you want, no one is so stupid that you can't see that God is real, they put God on the back burner and go sin, it took me two seconds to make a decision to choose God with my heart, and it's a process, I made the choice he made the change, I have always been different, and peculiar, I think God had chosen me long before I knew, I was sitting in MC Donald's one morning, I was so tired, I say God I need comforting please help me, he say look up, I saw two thin circle rainbows in the sky, all I could do was worship him, nothing or no one could have given me the peace I felt that fast, God is the answer for every situation amen. This lady came up to me, I never saw her before, she say God is telling me to tell you about writing a book, all I could say was thank you God, I was in bed and I felt God next to me, I heard pages flipping, I ask someone what they thought it meant, she say maybe God want you to read a special scripture, but God spoke to me, you need to write the book, the enemy is trying everything to stop me, because its glorifying God in every way. resist him and he has to flee. amen. I remember some time ago I would go to this service station, and talk to the guy that worked there, he was a big flirt, but I knew God was up to something, I put up with him long enough, one day I said I want to pray for you, I kid you not he gave his life to God, amen, when God said he wanted me to dance, I hired the best dance teachers in town, none of them could teach me a dance, they tired, it didn't work. I met one teacher and she say, I can help you God want you to use the talent he gave you, no one can teach you, I thanked her and she was right. God gave us all a talent to be used for his glory, amen, I tried to start a church perfect place, a store front office all set up and ready for church, two powerful pastors came to preach for me, it was like God sent them, I had no money to give them, I would pass out flyers to welcome people, two guys I gave flyers to tried to break in one night, and they started stoking the place, I closed the church and started traveling again, this time I had very little money, had a full tank of gas and enough for one more fill, I looked in my purse and found an extra twenty, only God could have put it there for food, it was raining,I never like to drive in the rain and heavy traffic, I could not figure out how to work my defroster, my windows were cloudy. the sign say no stopping on the side of the road but, I had to, I could not see, the big trucks were speeding close to my car, for some reason I was calm, I finally got the defroster to working, but that was a very close call, I have been just about to every state, in shelters and on the street, I stopped counting the souls that were won, the healings and casting out demons, God is so amazing and he chose me it's unbelievable, I would not change my journey for anything, God never said it would be easy, but I will never leave you, He has moved all distraction out of my life, so it's just me and Jesus, no one really understand my walk, it is so out of this world, if you don't know him you will never get it, I used to tell God people are going to think I'm crazy, God say so you are worried about people that can harm the flesh but can't touch the soul, that's when I stopped caring about what people think and pray for them.my husbands been dead 18 years, it would be nice to have someone to help glorify the lord amen, women get taken advantage of, especially by mechanics, I had two over charge me, and made the problem worse, but God took care of each one, God says love your enemies pray for those that hurt you, I will repay said the lord, sometimes he takes care of them right before my eyes, and other times he will let me know later. I was walking down the street, I passed a lady and she came up to me and ask are you a minister? I felt something when you passed me, I say yes that was God you felt not me, he is so good, I was crossing the street and here come a young man, he ask, what are you doing all alone, he stood in the middle of the street and stopped all the traffic for me to cross, I was at a fashion show, there were no seats, but one of the ladies in charge found me a chair, and would not let anyone to close to me, I call that the favor of God amen. when I arrived in this next town, I met a lady, and she invited me to sleep on her couch, I did for a week and then it was time to get on the road again, my daughter was in college, I would always call her and let her know where I am and I'm ok, when I called she says to me, mom I am tired of the dooms why don't you come here let's get an apartment together, I really couldn't believe my teenager wanted her mother to live with her, I was so excited, I had no belongings, so I left the next day, she was only three hours away, when I got there, we lived in her doom for two weeks while looking for an apartment, we used an apartment locator, he found the perfect place . we moved in by the end of the month, in a few weeks we were settled in and everything was in place, very nice, my daughters college was not far away, she left for school one morning, I was sleeping in, and I heard God speaking to me, he say go look in her closet in a shoe box, I say God I don't pry in her stuff anymore, she's grown now, I'm over that, but I obeyed God and went to the closet, I saw at least fifty shoe boxes, God say this one, I reached for it and it feel on the floor, there were no shoes in it, a lot of papers fell on the floor, I started to picked them up, and I notice court document headings, it got my interest, I started to read, my daughter's had a baby and has given it up for adoption, all the contact information was there, I started to pray what should I do God, he say dial this number, I got the child protective services the right office, this lady that answer act as if she knew me, she says hello we have been trying to get in touch with you, when can you come to see us? I was ready to go right now, she say what about tomorrow morning, I got there early, I went in her office, she say your grandson is in a foster home, I can take you to see him he's very cute, I say if he's mine I know he is, she say have a seat there were complications, he was born with just a brain stem. God spoke in my ear and said, but I have healed him, I felt God's present all over me, so we left going to the foster home, and she was telling me yes you can adopt him, you will be just fine, we got there, we walked in, one of the workers was holding him in a way I didn't like, he was just scamming, she gave him to me, he took a long look at me nonstop, and slowly stop crying, he knew who

I was, he was, perfectly normal, he was not supposed to be able to see or hear, his head was supposed to be very large, God had healed him like he said. This was one miracle after another, I broke down, I was full of God's glory, here this beautiful angel, it's a miracle. the foster mother was on vacation, they were telling me that she is a demon, she will fight you for your own child, they say she put feeding tubes in all the children, that way she get more money, she can drug them and don't have to be bothered with them, they sleep all day, I didn't want to believe any of it, I thought how can she keep my child from me, well she came back, and I found out every bit of it is true, she told me I had to leave she would make me a schedule, two days a week, I heard she ask them if I wanted him, of course I want my son, all of her family worked there, and they were all evil, she had young kids working there that just didn't care, and had no experience with children. he was six weeks old and in the mist of strangers, he cried all day and night, he never got a real bath, it was cold in their bathroom, they say he is fussy, no he's cold, they had his crib next to an open fireplace, it was cold. the older kids would run by and shake it, he never got any peace, when I came to visit I would hold him, he would talk baby talk to me and tell me his pain, remember he is not supposed to be able to talk, everyone would stop what they were doing and watch us, one lady said are you sure he was born with just a brain stem? Some would make fun and say no she healed him they refuse to believe in God so I just let it go. He would look at me and smile when I held him he would fall asleep and rest. I have never seen a baby as beautiful as he is. One lady told me he is tough, I said thank you God I know you are with him amen. The foster mother would lie to the doctor's about all the kids conditions, and he go along with it, they were all in it together, that's how she got to put feeding tubes in all of them, can you believe all the children need feeding tubes how evil. He was always drugged, one of the workers told me she put salt in his food all I could do was pray. I had no say she said I couldn't care for him anymore. They would never give him water I think it was because anything I wanted they were against it. I would ask if he had water today. he had the hiccups so bad he would get sick, one time his diaper was stuck to his bottom with poke in it, he had diaper rash very bad, unary track infections, he had a cold and the doctor gave her something that she would put up his nose, it was very painful for him, he would cry so hard, one time he let out a sound that told me I'm tired please help me, I was leaving him my time was up, and something say look back, when I did one of the workers was shaking him, all I could do was cry out to Jesus, I would have to leave him that way, sometime his little body would be so cold, no blankets to cover him up, all I could do was pray. The other kids there liked me, they would tell me how they couldn't sleep and they didn't want to be there, all I could do was pray, one of the workers was changing his diaper and he was groaning, I could feel him saying please stop hurting me. God kept me strong, 0nly he could have done it, praise you father, they would leave him in his crib and let him cry all day, I was following one of the workers in my car, she was taking him to the doctor, she would make turns and try to loose me, they were all in it together. CPS the attorney's the doctors the D A. I had no one that cared they started playing games, the foster mom and CPS. I knew that they would not let me have him. I call different agencies somehow they knew about me, they just laugh at me. I would call the abuse hot line. they knew about me, so I had no one. they were all in it together, it was Christmas time. I had bought the biggest teddy bear for him I drove over to give it to my baby. I knocked on the door, they came to the door and said its Christmas you can't come in, I just turn and walked away, again God was holding me in his arms, One time he had a scratch on the side of his eye, he had bags under his eyes and they were black, an infant, I say please help me Lord. he love his bottle, he burp like a man, it was so cute. I know God was holding both of us especially me, I was always an overly protective mother, and grandmothers you know our grandbabies are very special to us, he look just like us, more like his mother, they did not want to hear anything about God. They ask me to stop bringing my bible everyone didn't want to hear the bible. God was on his throne all the way, I went in one day, the baby was very sick, I couldn't take it I called the police, the ambulance showed up she had not fed him, he was hungry she wanted him to lose weight so she could tell the doctor he's not eating anymore, they investigated the place ask for records, this was the beginning of exposure of her abuse, the baby and I were sent there for a reason, neither one of us could have survive if God was not in it. the mother was so upset with me, she said not to set foot on her property ever again, but that didn't stop God he wasn't done yet. They started treating him a little better but not for long, they wanted him to be a vegetable. but God had healed him he was normal, and beautiful. it says on his medical records maybe he was misdiagnose all his test are normal. Somebody help me please amen, and when I look at him he reminded me of baby Jesus a miracle from God. I would go to different churches for prayer. I would pray and cry out to him please help me Jesus, I still have one of his diapers from when I first saw him. We had a bond you could see Gods presence when I held him. he was so peaceful and happy, when I leave they say to me the next day he never stop crying. I would ask questions, and the mother's husband would tell me your pushing it, they felt threaten by me they couldn't figure me out. I called my brother just to talk to someone, He told me to get an attorney and go get the baby, I got a job to make money to pay for an attorney, and I took my brothers advice I hired an attorney, he didn't seem interested or cared. I keep looking no one wanted to take the case, everyone in that town knew about that foster home, she had everyone fooled, When I first met some of the workers, they all told me they had tried to report her many times, but no one would listen. I talk to a new attorney, he took the case and my money but never filed with the courts, I had to take him before the board to get my money back. I found another attorney. He took the case, and started working on it. and I found out the pastor that ordained me is a RN, she offered to go to court with me, it would be good to help take care of the baby, I found a pediatrician for him, to show the judge he will be in good hands, the only lady that tried to help, at the foster home came to talk to the attorney, she told him how the baby acted when I was there, and he would cry all the time when I left him, he didn't give her much attention, I found out that he had been talking to the foster mother and CPS so they were all in it together, we went to court the Pastor came with me, the foster mother had the DA the doctor CPS and all her family there, this was the first court appearance, the judge talked in my favor I felt pretty good. they had told her I was sick. I needed help, because I say I healed the baby, I stop trying to tell them that I am not God I can't heal, they would do anything to make me look bad, the judge told the mother to release the babies records to me and she was going to give me the baby, they wanted the judge to think I was not capable of taking care of the baby. they could see he was healed but they wanted him to be sick, they hated me, she didn't want me to have my own grandson, I met a lady that invited me to her church, I felt very comfortable there, she was very concerned, I was just sitting in service with her and a lady came up to me and said, you are going through something give it to God you can't do it alone, one other Sunday in service a lady came and said to me, lady Satan is trying to kill you, amazing how God works, we had a second court date, the pastor wasn't with me. so I hired a nurse from an agency, hoping the judge would be pleased, our second court date was awful God told me to look over at the foster mother, I saw red fire in her eyes, God say that's Satan he never won anything, there's no one like you Lord. We had a different judge, different court room, and CPS and the foster mother had called my attorney, who was never on my said from the beginning, so the judge rule the baby stay in the foster home. my attorney never said one word to me. he went directly to the foster mother, and the rest including the nurse I hired. I went to the restroom when I returned the nurse I hired was talking to the mother, and all of them. God was holding me in his arms. I walked out of the courtroom I know he was going to work it out somehow in his own timing my faith was in him because he's the one that told me about my grandson from the beginning. I knew he had a purpose and a plan, or there would be no way I could have stood the pain. the pastor stayed on the phone with me all night. I still had my visitation rights. My next visit the husband was talking to a lady about the feeding tube, I wasn't paying much attention, and I heard God say listen, they are going to put the feeding tube in your son. the next visit it will be done, but walk by faith not by sight, my next visit was my last, the tub was in him, this big beautiful baby had a feeding tube. she would not feed him, so he would lose weight, and tell the doctor he wouldn't eat, what kind of doctor would do such a thing, knowing a baby is healthy. I guess the same kind of doctor that would aboard an unborn baby. He got sick a few times because of it. I picked him up and it was the saddest thing I have ever seen in my life. He was coughing and choking, sucking for his bottle, one of the ladies look over at me and started to cry, I knew God was with me he, had already told me. and then God say I will take over from here, leave and don't come back, the pastor called and said you need to leave, confirming what God said, I went back to my home town, I fell on my face and cried out to God Jesus please help me, he told me to go turn on the TV as soon as I did someone said on a talk show. God say angels wings are wrapped around the baby. I know it came from God. the peace I got can only come from him, later I call one of the nurses that work at the foster home she say your grandson has been adopted to a beautiful couple, and I am so happy, this is the same nurse that said she would help but turned on me. I called CPS and ask them where is my baby, they said you lost your rights we can't tell you anything, once again my faith in God kept me going, a couple of weeks later. a friend I met that invited me to her church down there called me, she say what is the name of the foster home your grandson is in? when I told her she say it's all over the news, it has been closed down, the mother and her husband are under investigation, they have removed all the kids, the police found mercury in a bottle, and the older kids were being molested, I notice God removed my child before all this happened to safety. My faith is still strong in the Lord, if he had not sent my child there. she and her husband would still be harming children, and babies, God always know what he's doing, so all alone I knew God said you are going all over the world and tell your story, and there is no story without the baby, He used a prophet to tell me what was going to happen, he use a beautiful lady to tell me there is something God want you to do. he used a co-worker to draw me to him, and two angels to love me and surrender to him. an infant to stop the abuse. God will tell you what is going to happen, and carry you in his arms though it, and show you the victory. there is no way I could see a child go through that and not hurt myself or someone else. I will just be honest. all I did was try to minister to those people. God you are awesome amazing and good. I adore you with all my heart. There is no one like you all we need is you God. no one can give peace that surpasses all understanding. he used a pastor to train me. He took me aside to himself and taught me everything I know. he knew when I said that prayer at Betty's house sitting on her couch that I meant it with all my heart. I gave him my life. I gave him full control, and from that point on I denied myself. all generational curses were broken. he covered me with his blood. He made me whole. A friend call me and said meet him at the church. I want to baptize you. how great is our God amen. The book of Nahum is all about how I had to deal with the wicket people in the foster home and how God exposed them forever, it will not come back a second time. The deep dark places. the shelters it doesn't get any darker than that, now the victory is in the making, people tell me he's adopted, and I say that just make God's story more beautiful, so you think that's going to stop God. just wait on him he has shown it to me, I was going on my morning walk, and I saw a little brown rock bouncing up and down, and I heard footsteps, I started looking all around over and over,and I heard God say it's me. halleluiah to the lame of God, so I kept walking, I went a long distance and he went with me all the way, and back, a real unusual beautiful sound, the next morning on my walk, I heard the same steps. I started to look around again, and God say if you keep looking I will stop walking with you, and I said ok God I'm sorry, he did not go the whole walk this time, praise your mighty name Lord, You are worthy to be praise, I would listen to a song over and over, it's called if it's goanna get done you will have to do it, so the world will know it, and see your power though it I misplaced it, and I was looking all over for it, a few weeks later God say right here your song, he put it right on the front seat of my car, only you Lord thank you. I was sitting on my couch watching TV all of a sudden I looked up on my book shelf there was this bright light, beautiful shades of the rain bow colors, I couldn't move it was shaped in a rectangular ultra lucent colors so bright it could blind you, it had brown dots on it, and lines dividing it, It moved upward. There was a thin circle shape rain bow on the entry way wall, the most beautiful color I have ever seen, and it was coming from the peep hole in my front door. it was about 4PM and it stayed there until 6pm, every day. I knew it was God I felt his presence. The next day it was there again, only there was more, I saw people facieses and different shapes of something. I saw, a lot of people gathered in this place, maybe a church; I saw someone holding a child in short pants and suspenders. The next day it was there again. It came for two weeks straight. I called this girl I know and told her. I had to release it too much to hold inside if I was out I made sure I got home in time. I say God what does this mean? the girl I told about it called me the next day, and said God said to tell you to read Isaiah 60. I go thank you Lord. You are an awesome God. the next week or so the brown dots in the circle turned into people, and the most special moment of all. God's face appeared on the very narrow part of the bookshelf, and later, I saw him sitting on his thrown. the rainbow in the hall way stayed there the whole time. I tried to take pictures they would not develop. I'm sure this was just for me. now God said go outside and look in the sky. I would see people walking in heaven, once I saw a lady in her kitchen and a child playing on the floor. In a different apartment I saw signs and visions all over my wall in beautiful bright eye blinding rainbow colors, different shapes and designs they moved across the wall from the living room to the bedroom. The shapes were just out of this world, there were rainbows all over, even in the kitchen sink, on the carpet in the bathroom. This happened every day same time I wasn't able to take pictures all I could do was look and praise him on my knees. I see rainbows all the time in my car once on my thigh. one other apartment more signs and visions I saw a cross in my closet, a rainbow, bright colors and designs on the ceiling a rainbow on the floor and all white designs all over the walls moving around. a thin rainbow on the wall, and one on the blinds that separated the living room from the bedroom. the white designs moved in to the kitchen. the two thin rainbows I believe were conformation because God had just told me about my husband. I had just walked inside and the first thing I saw was the two rainbows and I said thank you Lord. this last apartment I was in, I did take pictures I believe because God want the world to know. and some were white, all over the walls the ceiling the stove, the bathroom, the bedroom the fire place, the floor, the furniture, the door, here are some of the images amen. I still see rainbows sometime in my car they seem to follow me. I would not change one thing it has been long and difficult. but God never said it would be easy. but he will never leave you or forsake you, put all your trust in him. do not be afraid, no weapon formed against you will prosper. I look back and I can't believe I drove so many places for so long with very little money and always managed to find the shelters, and all the souls that were won, and I never approached any of them God sent them to me now I know it was all God not me. he gets all the glory. he told me in the beginning not to worry about myself doing anything, he was just using me. he took an insecure very shy person and turned my life around. I believe we were all put here for a purpose, if we give our lives to God with our whole heart. he will reveal it to you, he gave us all a talent to be used for his glory, without God we are just existing, you will go around in circles and never find true peace and meaning for your life, everything we have come from God even our children, we need to be humble and grateful. God give and he take away. I get so tired of people yelling yes I'm a Christian. I say please tell me what do you mean. they say I go to church and I pray. I go good you can't serve two masters. you will love one and hate the other people think severing the Lord you will have to give up all your things, God is the one who gave you your things, it's ok to enjoy them as long as we do not put them before God. we are not to be in love with things, they can't give you breath are heal you, and besides you can't take them with you when you die, things will come and go. but God is forever. and if you commit yourself to God they become less important to you. all you will need is God. you become like him. he is love. all you will want to do is love one another. and be a blessing to someone. before I met the lord I can remember, I always had a white couch, a grand piano,my kids used to say every space in the room is filled with something, and why we can't we sit on the couch why did you buy it. yes I was in love with things. I know God gave me a gift to decorate. people were so jealous back then they would copy everything with an attitude. and never gave me a compliment. Yes friends God is real all those things make me sick to look at them now, they are a distraction, if I do accumulate anything I don't keep it very long. I pass it on and bless others. I don't hold on to anything worldly. I bless others not with things I don't want, what reward is there in giving your junk to people. God always give back so much more. when God put his spirit inside of you, we become like him, all you want to do is love, be there for each other. God says if you are going to follow him you must deny yourself pick up your cross and follow him. We are not capable of doing these things. God knows your heart if you are striving to do right with all your heart. he comes in and change us and protect us. we make the choice he makes the change, theirs so much evil in the world. we need to realize that this is not our home. one day we will stand before the judgment of God. he see everything he never sleeps or slumbers the conclusion of the matter; obey God and keep his commands for this is the will for all man, every secret thing will be reveal whether good or bad. You cannot be in you right mind and not know that there is a God. If I can help you I will but, I can't put up with foolishness, God told me I had to be bold, I'm sending you in the world with wolfs and demons and was he ever so right. what does it profit a man to gain the world and loose his soul, seek and you shall find, knock and the door will be opened. The Lord knows all about your hurt and pain, there is nothing too big for God. all who are thirsty come to him and drink. you will never thirst again. he loves us so much he gave his only son to die on the cross for our sins. Why can't we live for him, none of us are perfect. We all fall short, but God knows your heart. He won't let us get tempted to do wrong. We have to give our lives to him to control and nothing can harm us amen. He wants us all to spend eternity with him. he gives us all the opportunity. Every morning we wake up is another chance to get it right. He has given me a glimpse of heaven and hell they are real. I hear some people tell me I'm in hell right now. I say but you can get out of this hell you're in now, but once you take that final breath it's too late and the bible says only God know the day and the hour we will die tomorrow may be too late. We need to realize how blessed we are, look around us and think back to where God brought us from. He says come as you are, it doesn't matter what you have done he will clean you up, our problems are blessings sometime the only way we learn is through our pain. It will make us stronger and bring us closer to God. He is also building character in us we only go through our problems they won't last forever. we need to let our light shine if we meet a hurting person what they need is Jesus, love never fails. I meet a lot of sick people, many think because their skin tone is different, that means they are better than others, no need to stoop to their level, show them the love of God he made us all the same, and he look inside our hearts not outward. we will answer to God for everything. so don't be rude. God say love those who hurt you. pray for them. He will repay, and I tell you he can do a much better job. He says touch not my anointed one's sometimes he will let me see him repay. there is no pleasure in seeing it, but it is good to know that God means what he says. I called a TV show just to voice my opinion, and the pastor answered, he said to me, I never answer this phone, but God said to answer an angel was calling. after we talk, he said a prayer that led me right into teaching me how to speak in tongues. look at God his ways are not like the world. you will never be able to figure him out, why try. he is perfect. everything he does is for our own good amen. Just be obedient keep his commands. nothing can harm you. Here are two beautiful stories I like to share. the first one is about a man that was involved with the mafia. He lives in a beautiful mansion. he's into drugs; he had a big fence around his mansion that would shock anyone that came near it, he had a vicious dog also, one day a lady walked up to his house and the gate opened, the dog started licking her, she walked straight to him. he could not believe how she got inside, she begin to tell him she was sent by God to set him free, she prayed with him, he accepted the lord, that was the end of his old life. this was very true. he was on TV telling his story, still in shock about it amen. This other story is about this couple getting a divorce. the husband wanted out of the marriage. His wife never worked, and she never paid bills, without him she would be lost, well he left, they had two boys, and for some reason she did not get the house; he left them with nothing. somehow she managed to find a job. it was thanksgiving holiday. She found a small apartment. She could not afford to buy food. one of the neighbors knock on her door, and said, I will be alone for thanksgiving dinner, I would like to invite you and your children, she was so happy for her boys, dinner was beautiful, she even brought left overs home. a few days later she wanted to return the dishes back to the lady, she went to her apartment but there was no answer, after the third time, she went to the office and ask about the lady, the manager told her the apartment had been empty for three months, she was in shook. God sent an angel to bless the mother and her two boys. a true story. this was on TV also. God can do all things. I was in my car driving down the road and I heard God say to me, I really did suffer and died on that cross, I said Lord thank you for choosing me, a sinner, and loving me the way you do, He is no respecter of person, he loves us all, when you deny yourself, surrender all to him, you can have a personal relationship with him, he knows your heart, if you are serious, he knows what we are going to do before it crosses our minds. I was telling this one guy, God is holding us though our pain, but he says, it doesn't make it easier. I go who cares if God's holding you it doesn't matter what's going on. In this world we will have troubles but take heart I have overcome the world amen, and we are just going though, it won't last forever, we can do all things though Christ who strengthens us amen. Without faith it is impossible to please God. I was driving down the road one day and I was listening to the oldies but goodies music, this was a long time ago, which is something I never do, it is always Christian music or nothing, and I heard God say, so you are not listening to my music anymore, I quickly changed back and said I am sorry Lord. I wrote letters to many different pastor's about my grandson. I was in so much pain, I even wrote president and the governor. I did get a call from the governor's office, only one pastor answered back, and I did not have his address so I called for it, it was very easy to connect to his staff and office, I have always liked him he does not beat around the bush, I was very excited to receive his letter it really did help me a powerful man of God. If you are tired, discouraged and you have tried everything to fix your situation, drugs, alcohol, sex, things, and nothing is changing, your answer is in God. He wants to give you rest, and peace, just say this prayer, God forgive me of my sins, come into my life, I believe Jesus died for our sins. amen. Now tell him yes, I am tired lord. I want to know you better is it true you can take ashes and make something beautiful, find a good church if possible go to revival, show God you are sincere with your heart, he will come in and make you a new creation. old things will pass away, get a bible, you will never be the same amen this is my prayer I say every morning, trust in the lord with all your heart and lean not on your own understanding, but in all your ways acknowledge him and he will direct your path. fear not for I am with you be not dismayed for I will strengthen you, yes I am your God, I will help you, I will uphold you with my righteous right hand. Those that wait on the lord will renew their strength they will soar high on wings like eagles they will run and not go weary they will walk and not faint. If you are not paying a price to follow God you are not following him close enough. People that God's going to used mightily he works with them for years and years. Love the lord with all your heart mind soul and strength. No weapon formed against me will prosper. if God is for me who can be against me. Lord I give you all honor and glory. I pray for the salvation of every lost soul, please forgive us when we complain, if we think back to where you brought us from and look around us, we are very blessed, and help us when we get consumed with the things of this world, we are nothing without you, anything else is just existing. I pray for all sickness and disease, hopelessness and addictions. the families that are involved in all the tragedies. Our brave soldiers, and their families, People that are incarcerated some are innocent, the elderly, many are lonely and abused, What God started he will finish so the best years of my life is yet to come. I pray for battered women, they fill trapped and think there is no way out, our policeman, fireman, medical emergency drivers and leaders of our country. our abandon babies are brought into this world, some are thrown into slathered house foster homes, and abused. some by their biological and adopted parents, I pray for all the wickedness in the world, the evil, cruelty, bitterness, envy, spitefulness and jealousy, you try to befriend them with words, they look at you strange, they look at each other,they never say a word. they laugh at you put you down to build themselves up, they love compliments but never give you one. they copy everything you do. In church every time the door open, Active in the church, take a front row seat, every time they open their mouths their quoting scripture, and never do one word of it or follow God, Lord heal touch guide and protect in Jesus name amen. Are you fornicating, Do you have an attitude? Do you steal? Are you angry? Do you gossip? Are you jealous? and you say you're Christian. I get bothered about that, either follow God or prepare to go to hell. We have no time to waste. He will meet you where you are. you can't serve the world and God. it's your choice I'm tired of it you know better. These two commandments are the most important one's love the lord with all your heart. love your neighbor as yourself, how can you sleep at night in a warm bed, and know there are many children living on the street hungry, if God has blessed you, please bless someone else. everything belongs to God. he give and he take away. a gift is not a gift until you give it away amen. love people, not things. happiness is not having what you want, happiness is wanting what you have, enjoy the little things, one day you will look back and realize it was a big thing. God loves us so much. he may let us bend, but he won't let you break. I am living proof. I have suffered most of my life, which I will talk about in my next book. I pray for people who hurt and use me, all they need is Jesus. How will they see him if I act the way they are. the bible says love them, God is love and love never fails. where much is given much is required, I wouldn't change my walk with God for anything, many are the affliction of the righteous, he has shown me where he's taking me, and he is carrying me every step of the way. I am praying for you, God is the truth the way the life. If you follow him all of your needs will be met, he will fight your battles for you. He will make your enemies your footstool. He will protect you. He will give you peace he has a plane and purpose for your life, all you will want to do is love one another no greater love than this. that a man lay down his life for his brother amen. you will be set free, you will have a personal relationship with God. that is his will for you. God had a perfect plane, when my daughter asked me to come live with her in college. I had an emergency C section with her. When I woke up my doctor was standing over me, and he said a miracle just happened. the coil was wrapped around her neck several times. My daughter still has the scar on her neck from it trust God he knows what he is doing. He is waiting for you amen. Everything the prophet said has happened, except the victory and I see it coming soon. I was out shopping I saw a lady and her baby the baby's eyes were very yellow. I ask the mother what is the problem, she say he has jaundice. I ask if I could pray for him. I didn't even touch him. I just started to pray. She thanked me and went on her way and I went my way, as I was walking away I felt power come from me. God say the baby is healed. I stared to run find them, but God say the baby is healed where is your faith? I said thank you lord, a lady came up to my car and just laid on it. I ask if I could help her. She said CPS has taking my children away. She was in very upset. I ask if I could pray for her, she gave her life to God, I said you will be ok now amen, I was at the gym. A lady started talking to me, and I said to her, it was nice meeting you, every time I tried to leave she would start to say more, after the third time God say it's her time go back. I prayed for her she accepted the Lord, she thanked me, and said I have never been in so much pain, and I said not anymore amen look at God. I worked in between trips little jobs, every day on break at this one place a soul was won amen. now I know I was there to win souls. This one job had I told everyone I was a minster. One lady said good there is one lady here that's going through a lot, when I met her she looked very worried and sad. The next morning when I walked in the office, she was sitting at my desk. I just started praying. She accepted the lord all I could do was praise and thank God, I never went back to that job amen. I was at a fast food place parked outside, and the manager came to my car and ask me if I was ok, she kept talking finally she started to tell me her problems. I ask if I could pray for her, she accepted the Lord, and she went back inside crying. God sent her to my car for rest amen. I met this lady at a department store parking lot. she walked over to my car. she was stuttering. she was ashamed to tell me she was sleeping in her car. She just walked right up to me she had trouble saying it I am sleeping in my car. She started to cry, I ask if I could pray for her and you know the rest thank you Jesus. I was in this town, and I ran into a girl I knew. she was excited to hear about my ministry. She says I wished my friend was here today she is having a very hard time. I ask when will she come back, She's off today tomorrow is good. I was leaving today, but I will sleep in my car tonight, and come back tomorrow. I met her the next day, and was she happy to see me. we started to pray. she broke down, she was in pain. After she gave her life to God she held me tight, and said thank you, I say it's God you are going to be ok now amen. I was downtown dancing for God, and here come the crowd, and I here God say over there. I looked, and I saw this young girl demon posseted very bad, I go over and her voice was deep. her face was scary. her parents were circling the block waiting for her. She couldn't move God had her I started to pray, she gave her life to God, and it was all over, she was healed, her face looked like an angel her voice was normal. she walked to the car and left. I was on the road headed to another state out in the desert no one insight, and here come a trucker, he tried to run me off the road, over and over. I didn't know what to do then I say, what am I thinking, God he is messing with me, before I got me out, I heard a loud sound, he had two blow outs, not one but two, and he was right in front of me moving slow, all the rubber went on the side of the road, none touched my car. Touch not my anointed one's amen. The next state was having a bad storm, everything had closed down. All the lights were out. I was the only one out. I was living in my car then. I parked at a store, and fell fast asleep in the back of my van. I heard a knock on my window it was security asking me to come inside. it took him a long time to wake me up, the light that is always over me was there even in that storm. I had nowhere to go, it was freezing, but God was there. One night an angel walked around my car very tall deep voice, and one walked right by my car, sometime they just stare and walked away out of sight. God sends them often. I still can't believe I had my daughter trail me in her car to her first college, a thirteen hour drive. I must have been out of my mind. We got to the college safe thank God, and we had problems with one of the ladies in the office. I made some phone calls. I got the connection and the president on the phone. He asked me what do you need I say I want to see you face to face, he laugh but made an appointment to see me the next day. he was very nice. he said the best thing to do is walk with you over to the office so they could see me with you, and that worked when they saw him they were shocked. I had no more problems with them I stopped at the gas station to fill up, and accidently hit a big red pole, red paint was all over my car I could not do anything right then, so I went inside to pay. I got back to my car, and two men were ripping the red paint off with some kind of cleaner. they never said a word. they cleaned until all the paint was gone. It looked so much better, they got in their truck and drove away they never said a word. I yelled out to them God sends angels. I walked into a store the man that waited on me was holding his face. He said he was in so much pain from a bad tooth he just started the job he got to wait 30 days for his insurance. I ask if I could pray for him. I touched his face he started to shake and he stud still and he looked at me, and ask where did the pain go I say it is gone God took it away you won't need to wait for your insurance you are healed amen. I had a job at a little dress shop and the owner's sister was driving up, she parked her car, and the owner ran out to her car with a shopping cart. She laid her sister across the cart she could not stand up alone she had back problems, they got in the shop, and God say touch and pray for her. I did she sat and talked for a while when she got ready to leave. she got up and ran to her car. The owner said to her slow down I say it's ok, God has healed her amen. One night in my car I looked and saw men walking in all brown. I was in one town and I would go visit this shelter. I didn't live at this one they had a good praise and worship band at the chapel. I would go dance and praise my pain away. I had just found out about my grandson. I love to danced it makes me happy, so God led me there. I met beautiful people we all danced. A lady invited me to stay at her home, and I did for a few days her friend came over to visit, both of them were very active in the church, they were there every time the door opened, they started abusing me in any way they could. the house had a light on the front door, so if any one came close the light would come on, one morning at about 3am the light started flashing very fast, I heard God say get out of here and do it now, praise God, how can you claim to know God and act that way. I stay away from people, unless I am led by God, yes people and churches. I get frustrated seeing how they use God. I will take you to heaven with me if I can help you, but I will not go to hell with you ok. I was low on gas, and I saw this pawn shop. I looked around in my car and found an old radio, the man that worked there say what are you trying to do? I say get gas money. he went in his pocket and gave me twenty dollars. This was in a state where no one gives away anything it was God I know. I had hernia surgery very painful. I had to recover on my own no one was there to help except one man in my apartments he helped as much as he could. God will always send someone. I was trying to get my strength back, so I took a walk down the hallway, and here come a man running and pushed me right into the wall. I thought I was going to die .the pain was so bad, but God is always with us this was no mistake he knew I just had surgery, but the bible says touch not my anointed ones, and do my prophets no harm. I went back to that complex later, and I ask about the man that pushed me. they say he's dead, he went to the hospital and never came back. God wanted me to know that. every one that has wrong me, are either dead, lost businesses, homes or struck with some kind of sickness. he always let me know this every time. If the world hates you keep in mind that it hated me first. If you belong to the world it would love you as its own, as it is you do not belong to the world but I have chosen you out of the world that is why the world hates you. Blessed are you when people insult you, persecute you, and falsely say all kinds of evil against you because of me, rejoice and be glad, because great is your reward in heaven, in the same way they persecuted the prophets before you Jesus said, whoever has my commands and obeys them, he is the one who loves me, he who loves me will be loved by my father and I to will love him and show myself to him amen. I was at a place trying to check into lodging, and met a lady. I started telling her about my ministry, and she offered to pay two nights for me, and she invited me to lunch. The next day she gave me a hundred dollar bill all I could do was give God the praise amen, God loves you so much, open up your hearts let him come in and give you peace and rest amen. I hope my story will help you, God is real. He is merciful and forgiving. He use people like me and others to show you don't turn away amen. I wrote a letter to the foster home trying to help them. I also wrote one to my grandson, He is 15 years old now the pictures are just some of the signs wonders and visions that appeared on my walls, there are many more, this is all God wanted me to show you, the rainbows come almost every day in my car and everywhere I go, and the light that follows me he never leaves me, so I will not fear. those who except my commandments and obey them, are the ones who love me, and because they love me my father will love them, and I will love them and reveal himself to each of them, all who love me will do what I say, my father will love them, and we will come and make our home with each of them john 14:20-21-23 It wasn't my daughter who wanted me to get an apartment with her, really it was God, for I know the plans I have for you declares the Lord, plans to prosper you, and not harm you, plans to give you hope, and a future then you will call on me and pray to me and I will listen. You will seek me and find me, when you seek me with all your heart, I will be found by you declares the Lord. I will bring you back from captivity. when we turn to him in wholehearted devotion, and abide in him, we will experience blessing and contentment even in the midst of difficulty amen. Jesus died for us lets live for him amen. my true brother and sister and mother are the ones that do what my father in heaven want, Please be ready for the coming of the Lord Amen., the rainbows appeared all over, In the bathroom the stove, the floor, the sinks, they were all over.

Dear Cody.

You are always on my mind. I think about your uncle who you remind me of so much you are indeed my special grandson. I feel your presence I know you feel mine. God is in charge you keep amazing everyone. All wrong will come to an end.

I Love You,
Grandma

I ask God to have mercy on all involved he will one day fulfill his plan to restore goodness permanently, but while we wait we must remember that revenge is not something we take into our own hands, God will punish those who deserve it in his own way and his own time. I will be happy to help in any way I can. I am writing to you as an ordained Minister. My calling is to win souls. This scripture from the bible, Ezekiel 33-7 says I have made you watchman for the house of Israel so hear the word I speak and give them warning from me when I say to the wicked O wicked man you will surely die and you do not speak out to dissuade him the wicked man will die for his sin and I will hold you accountable for his blood, but if you do warn the wicked man to turn from his ways and he does not do so he will die for his sin but you will have save yourself This why I must obey God. He sent his son into the world not to condemn it but to save it. God is so good and loving and forgiving he is waiting on us to turn to him for peace and freedom. God loves you he hate what you are doing I know my little grandson is beautiful and loving so is his mom and my other children. It is wrong to keep him from his family no one can love a child the way his own family can or take better care, without God I could not stand the pain. He is my only grandchild. Every time I see a baby my heart ache when I think about the lies you have told on him my heart ache, it is wrong to stop an innocent baby from enjoying his food to me it's a crime. I would take this very serious and not do it again and remove the ones that do not need it, God can clean you up and make you a new person. God will not let the guilty go unpunished

Pastor Heather Lynn

I

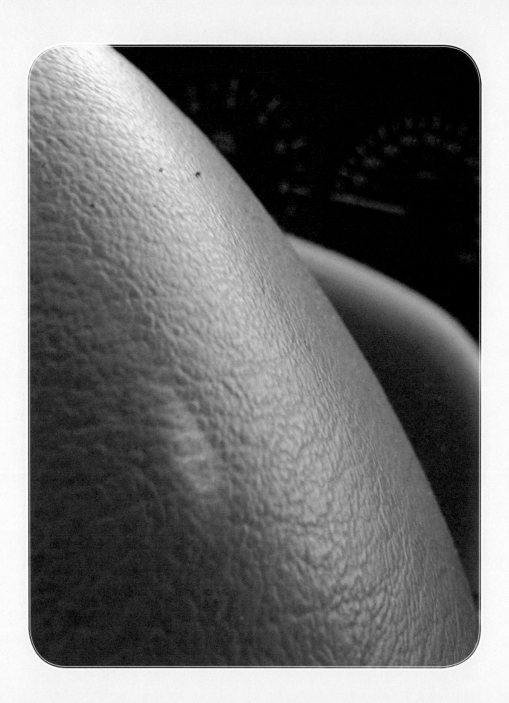

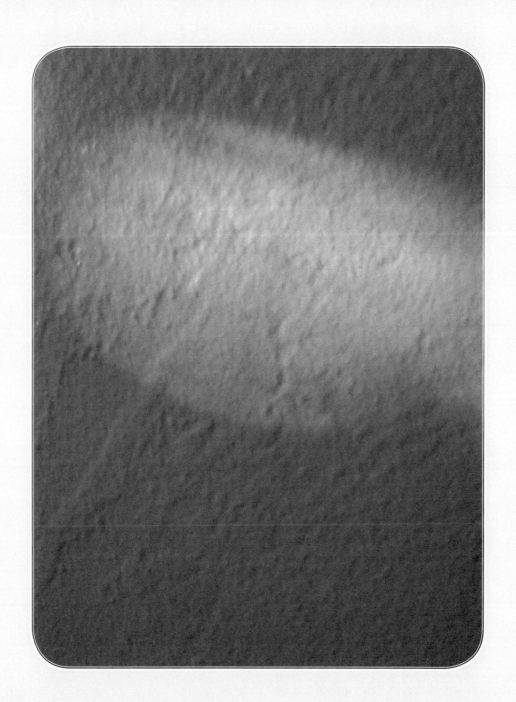

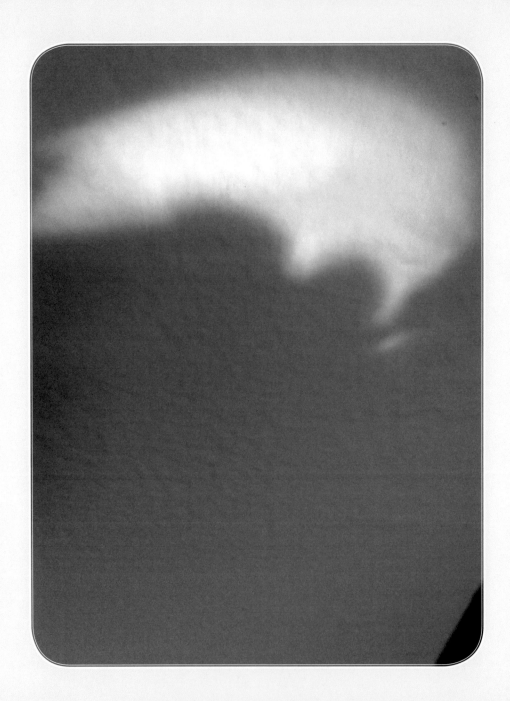

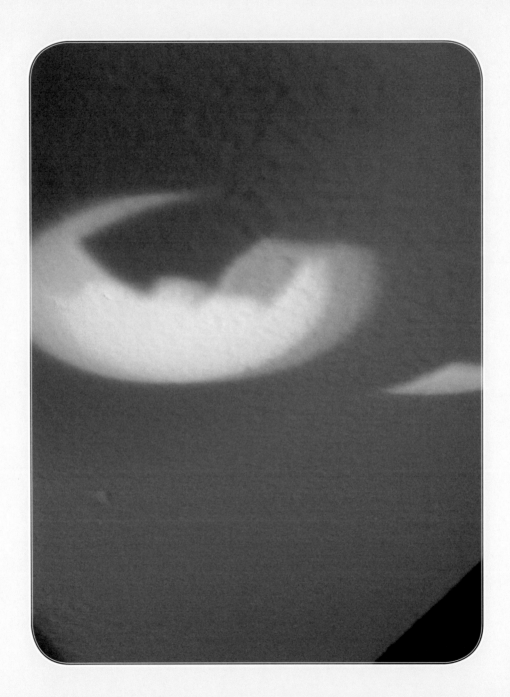

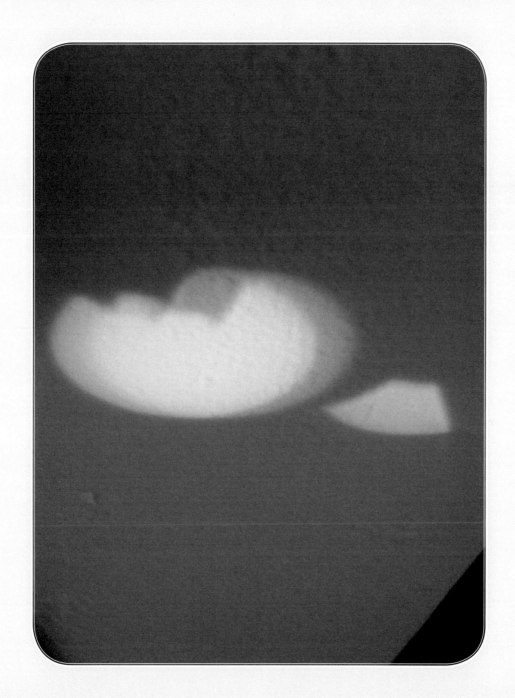

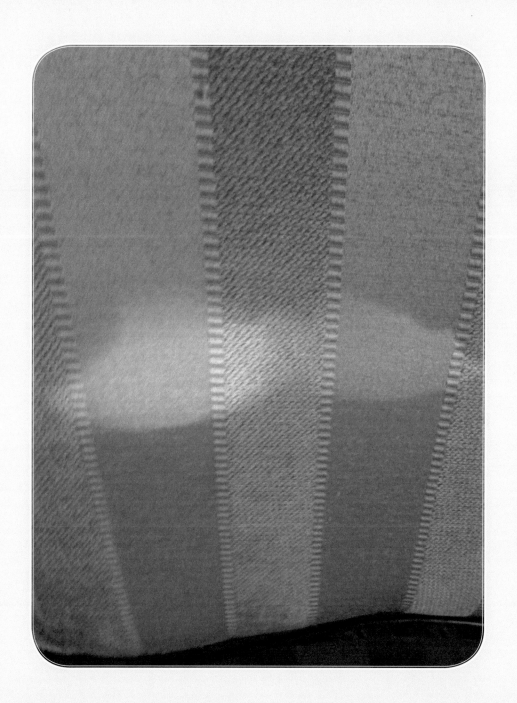

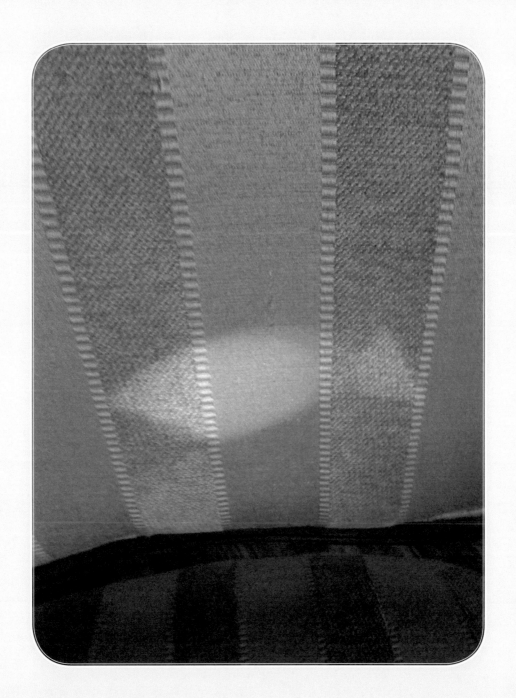

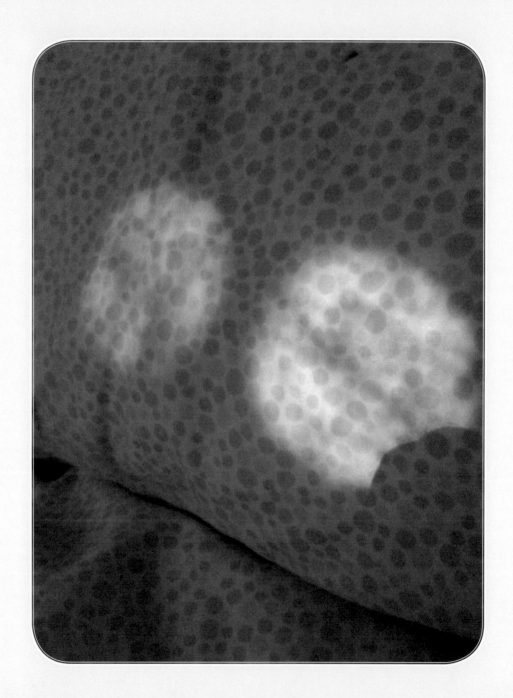

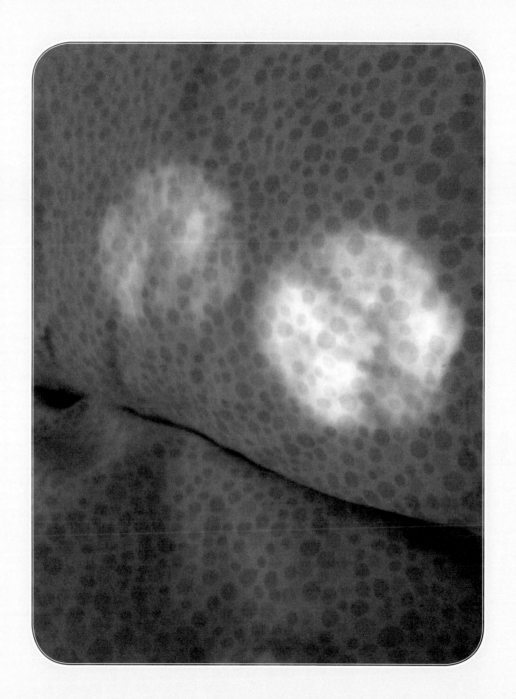

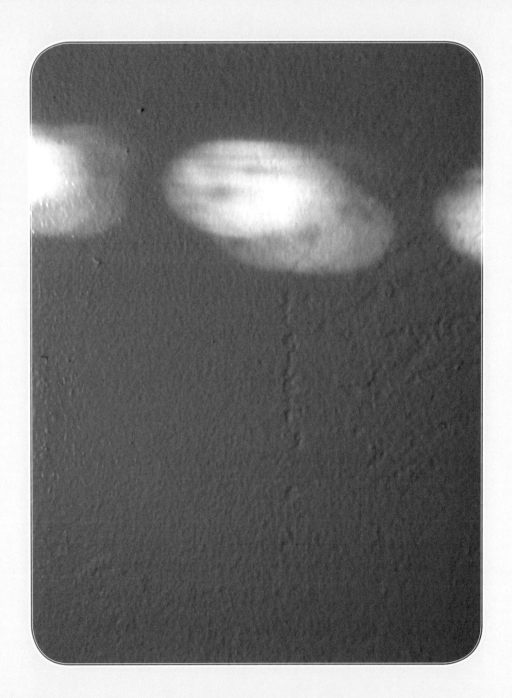

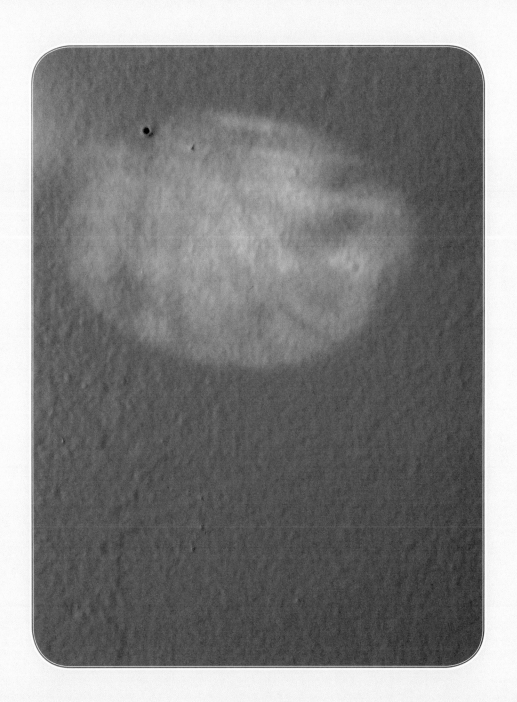

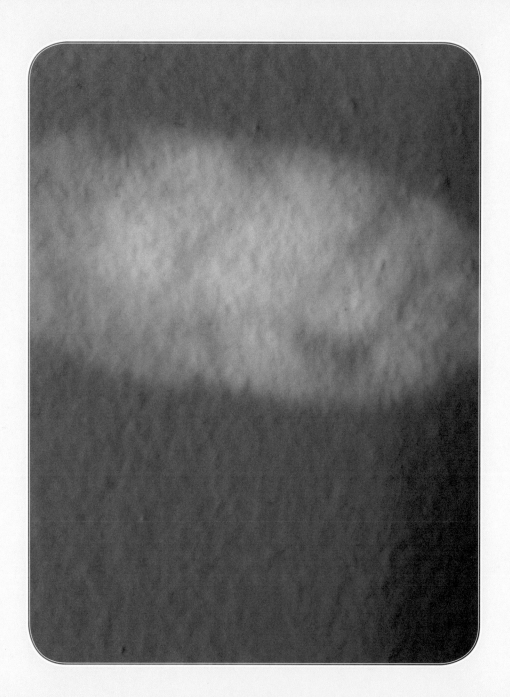

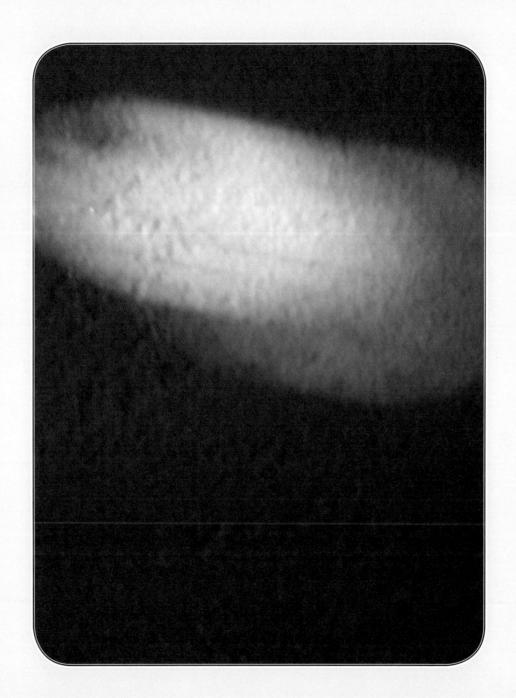

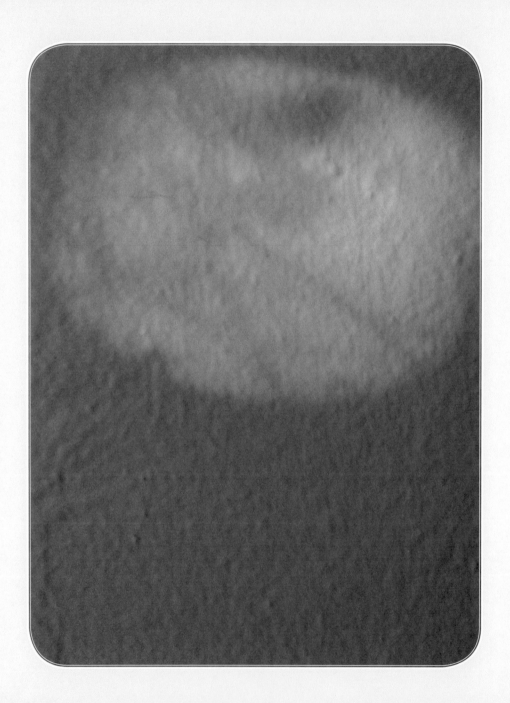

Printed in the United States
by Baker & Taylor Publisher Services